SHARKABET

A Sea of Sharks from A to Z

WestWinds Press®

In association with the American Museum of Natural History

SHARK! Just saying the word out loud gets your heart racing, doesn't it? Most people immediately think of the giant, bloodthirsty great white shark in the movie *Jaws* munching on helpless, screaming swimmers. But most sharks aren't nearly so terrifying.

Did you know there are more than 400 different kinds of sharks swimming in the waters of the world today? There are slow-moving harmless giants, swift savage predators, and even tiny glow-in-the-dark sharks. There are also more

than 600 kinds of rays, skates, and chimaeras (ky-MARE-ahs), which are close relatives of the shark.

Sharks, rays, skates, and chimaeras are all called cartilaginous (cart-eh-LAJ-e-nus) fish because their skeletons are made of cartilage—the same flexible stuff your ears and the tip of your nose are made of. That feature makes them different from the bony fish, which have skeletons made of hard bone like you and I do. Scientists also call cartilaginous fish by their Greek name, chondrichthyans (con-DRICK-thee-ans).

That big word means cartilage fish: *chondros* = cartilage + *ichthys* = fish. Bony fish are called osteichthyans (os-tee-ICK-thee-ans): *oste* = bone + *ichthys* = fish. The drawings on page 4 show the many differences between cartilaginous fish and bony fish.

In this book, I call *all* of the chondrichthyans sharks, to make it simpler.

People who study sharks are still deciding about how the many kinds of cartilaginous fish are related. There's even disagreement on what

THE SHARK FAMILY TREE

This handy Shark Family Tree shows the possible relationships among the cartilaginous fish. Notice how many groups are extinct.

WITH INPUT FROM DR. EILEEN GROGAN, DR. DICK LUND, AND DR. JOHN MAISEY

3

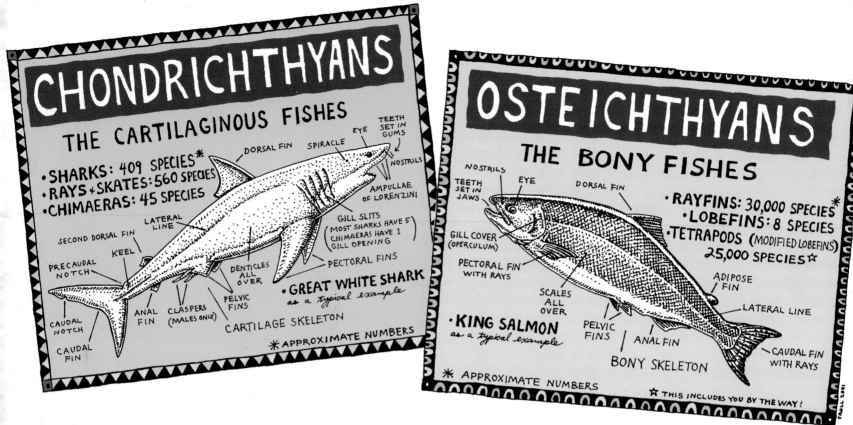

CHONDRICHTHYANS
THE CARTILAGINOUS FISHES

- SHARKS: 409 SPECIES*
- RAYS+SKATES: 560 SPECIES
- CHIMAERAS: 45 SPECIES

DORSAL FIN
SPIRACLE
EYE
TEETH SET IN GUMS
NOSTRILS
AMPULLAE OF LORENZINI
GILL SLITS (MOST SHARKS HAVE 5, CHIMAERAS HAVE 1 GILL OPENING)
LATERAL LINE
SECOND DORSAL FIN
KEEL
PRECAUDAL NOTCH
DENTICLES ALL OVER
PECTORAL FINS
• GREAT WHITE SHARK as a typical example
CAUDAL NOTCH
ANAL FIN
CLASPERS (MALES ONLY)
PELVIC FINS
CARTILAGE SKELETON
CAUDAL FIN
✳ APPROXIMATE NUMBERS

OSTEICHTHYANS
THE BONY FISHES

- RAYFINS: 30,000 SPECIES*
- LOBEFINS: 8 SPECIES
- TETRAPODS (MODIFIED LOBEFINS) 25,000 SPECIES ☆

NOSTRILS
TEETH SET IN JAWS
EYE
DORSAL FIN
GILL COVER (OPERCULUM)
PECTORAL FIN WITH RAYS
SCALES ALL OVER
ADIPOSE FIN
LATERAL LINE
• KING SALMON as a typical example
PELVIC FINS
ANAL FIN
BONY SKELETON
CAUDAL FIN WITH RAYS
✳ APPROXIMATE NUMBERS
☆ THIS INCLUDES YOU BY THE WAY!

---

a "true" shark is. See the Shark Family Tree on page 3.

Today's sharks had relatives cruising the oceans 400 million years ago, way before dinosaurs roamed the earth. Prehistoric sharks far outnumbered the bony fish in those days and came in many odd shapes and sizes. Some were so wild-looking it's hard to imagine that they were related to modern sharks.

Most of the creatures in this book have a scientific name and one or more common names. Most prehistoric sharks don't have common names, but I've taken the liberty of naming a few.

This alphabet book explores the world of living and extinct sharks and their cartilaginous cousins. Watch for the EXTINCT box that tells you which ones are no longer around.

If you're hungry to bite into more information on these cool critters, check out the back of the book. There's a section on Amazing Shark Facts and a Field Guide with more details on each shark.

So, on to the pictures! Here are my chondrichthyan favorites, one letter at a time.

Very sharkily yours,

Ratfish Ray

4

ANGEL SHARKS fly through the water with fins that look like tiny angel wings.

BULL SHARKS cruise the shores of jungle rivers
looking for an easy meal.

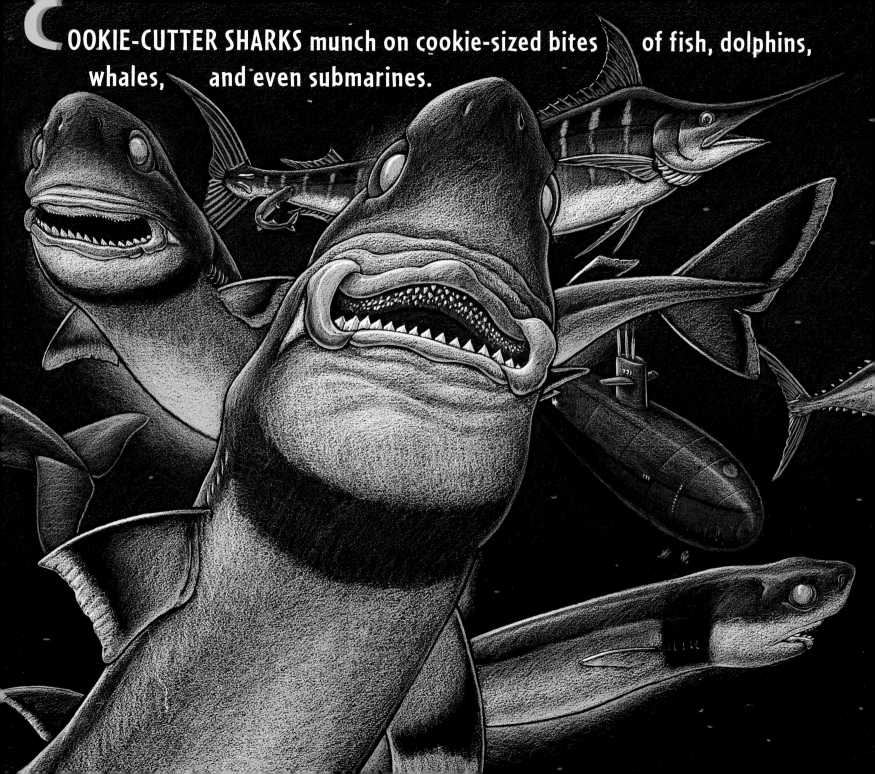

COOKIE-CUTTER SHARKS munch on cookie-sized bites of fish, dolphins, whales, and even submarines.

DOGFISH hunt and travel in packs, just like dogs.

ELEPHANTFISH use their funny-looking noses like radar to find their prey.

FRILLED SHARKS slink through the sea with eel-shaped bodies, snake-like heads, and triple-pronged teeth.

GOBLIN SHARKS would look right at home at a Halloween party.

HELICOPRION (hel-eh-co-PRY-on) ripped into its victims with a lower jaw shaped like a circular saw. Ouch!

EXTINCT

INIOPTERYGIANS (in-ee-op-toe-RIDGE-ee-an) not only looked like airplanes, but some scientists believe they could glide through the air. EXTINCT

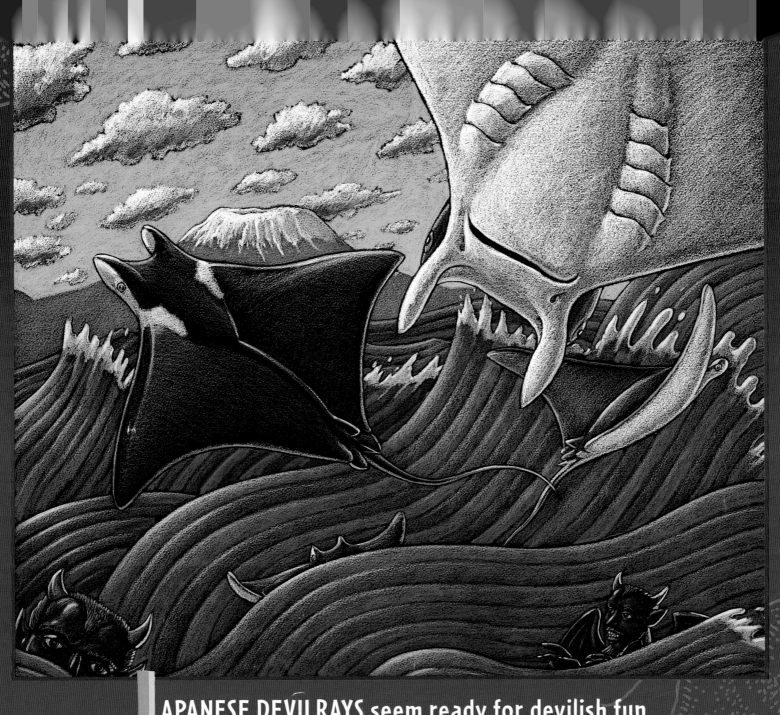

JAPANESE DEVILRAYS seem ready for devilish fun
and have the "horns" to prove it.

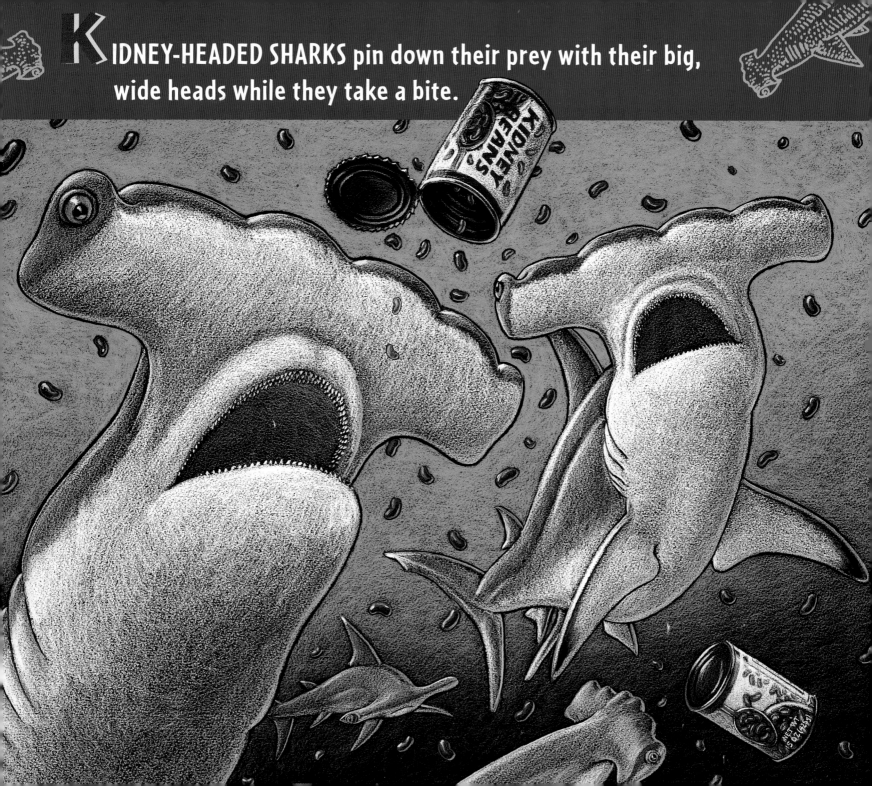

KIDNEY-HEADED SHARKS pin down their prey with their big, wide heads while they take a bite.

LISTRACANTHUS (list-ruh-CANTH-us) wore "armor" of long, jagged denticles from the tip of its nose to the end of its tail. EXTINCT

MEGALODON (MEG-eh-low-don) was a massive predator

that munched on 30-foot whales half its size.

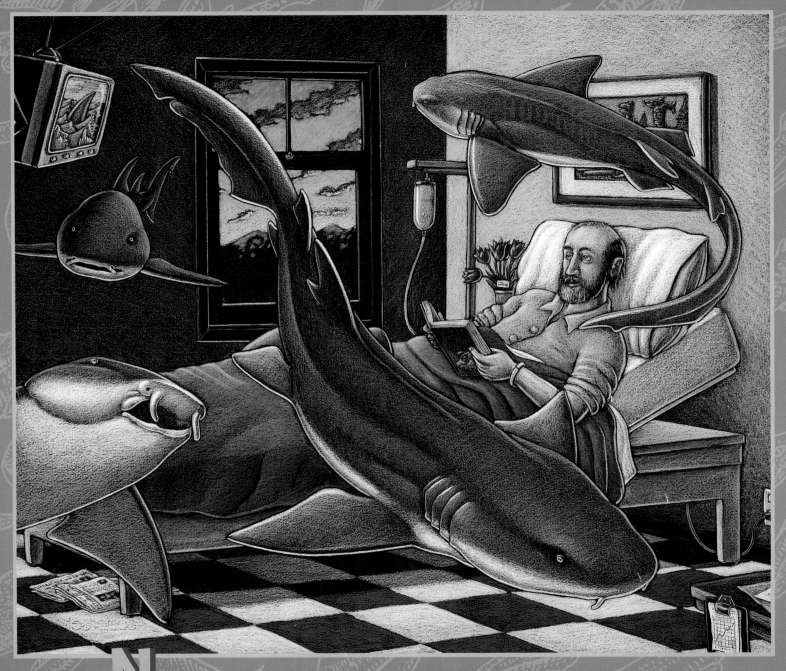

NURSE SHARKS won't take care of you in the hospital,
even in your wildest dreams.

ORNITHOPRION (or-ni-thoh-PRY-on) may have probed the sand with its lower jaw as it searched for a lunch of hard-shelled creatures.

EXTINCT

PETALODONTS (PET-al-oh-dahnts) were bizarre bucked-toothed beauties that lived long ago when Montana and Indiana were under water.

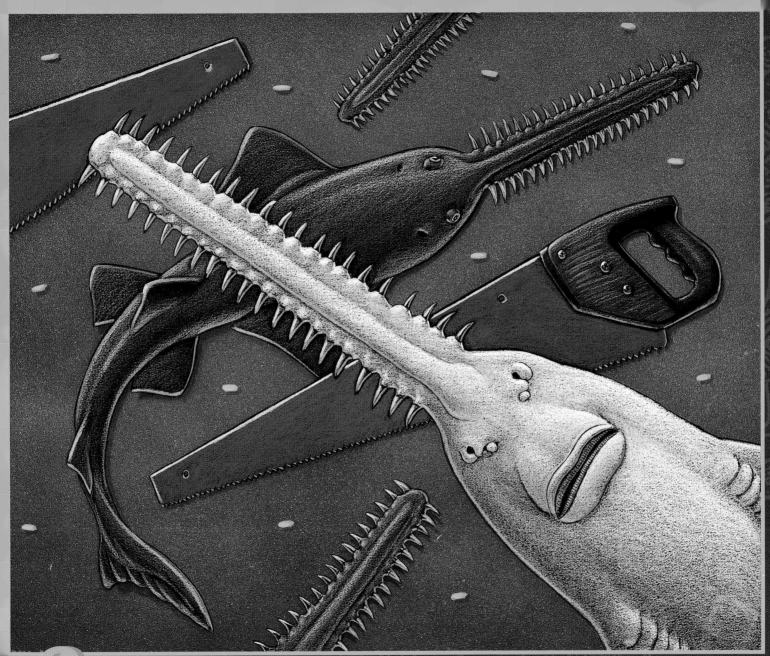

QUEENSLAND SAWFISH slash at their victims with saw-like snouts.

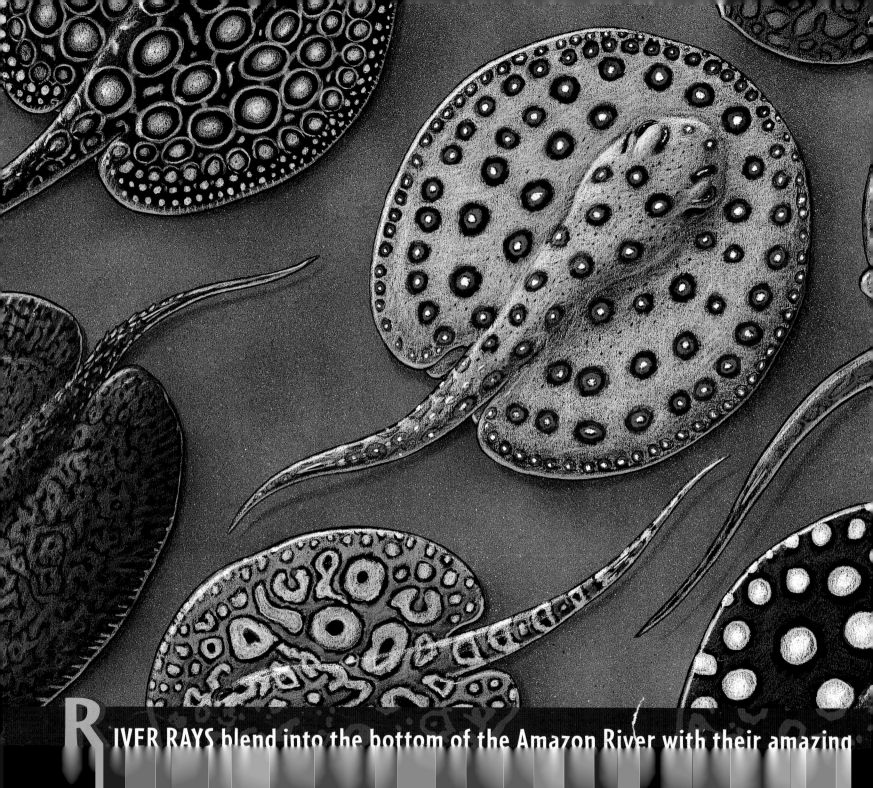

RIVER RAYS blend into the bottom of the Amazon River with their amazing

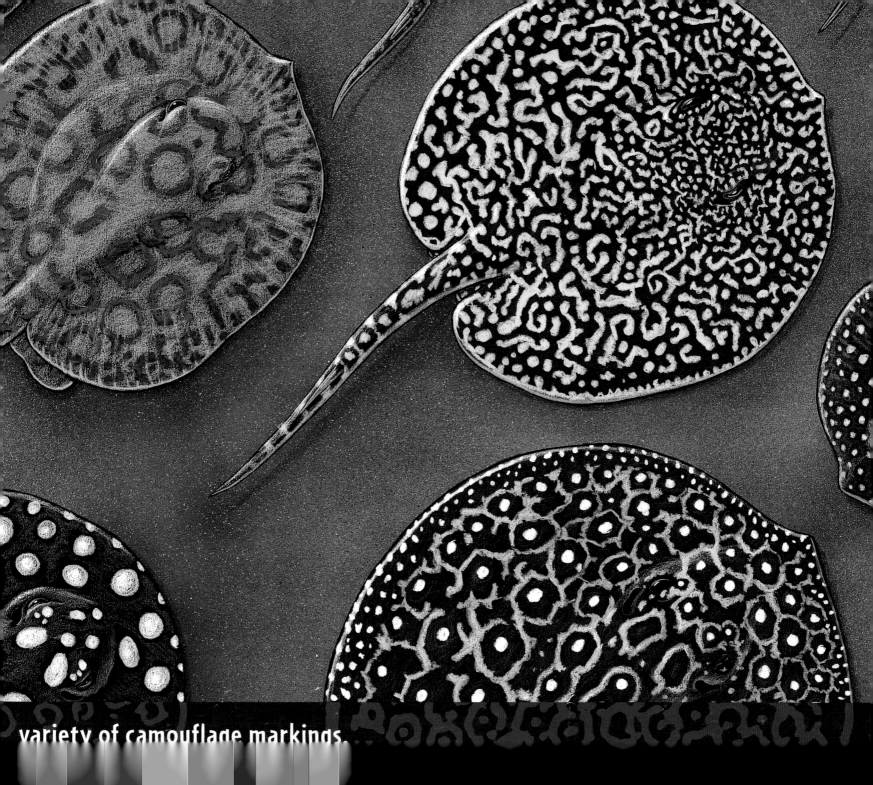

variety of camouflage markings.

SCISSOR-TOOTHED SHARKS sliced their prey neatly in two, like a gigantic pair of scissors.

THRESHER SHARKS stun small fish by cracking their incredibly long tails like whips. WHACK! SMACK! Yum.

UROLOPHUS (your-oh-LOAF-us) STINGAREES can sting a wader who's not paying attention. Watch where you step!

VARIED CARPET SHARKS spend a lot of time lying around on the ocean floor—just like colorful carpets.

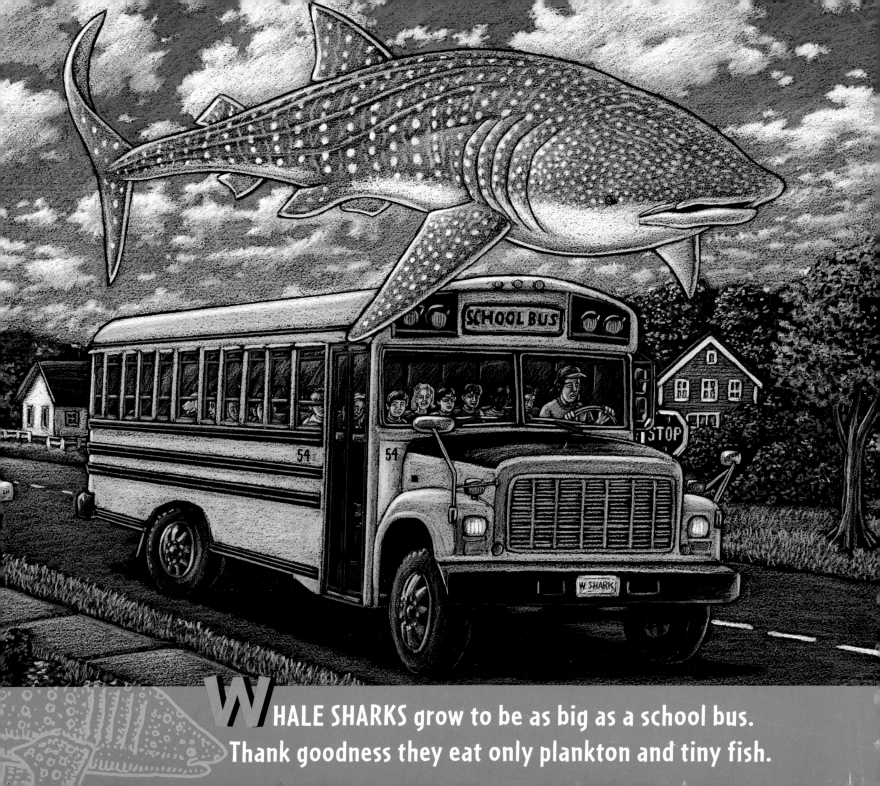

WHALE SHARKS grow to be as big as a school bus.
Thank goodness they eat only plankton and tiny fish.

XENACANTH (ZEEN-ah-canth) SHARKS terrorized prehistoric swamps all over the world 300 million years ago.

EXTINCT

YELLOW SHOVELNOSE GUITARFISH are shaped just like guitars.
Don't even think about trying to play one!

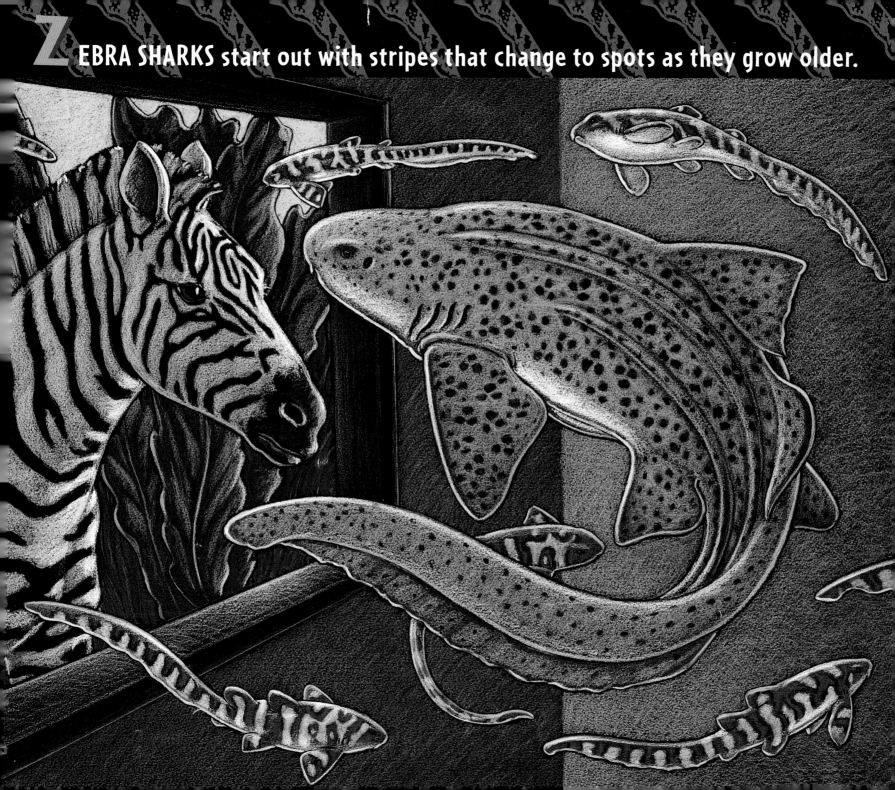

ZEBRA SHARKS start out with stripes that change to spots as they grow older.

COOL
SHARK
SHOW
THE
CARTILAGE
CROWD!

Bloodhounds of the Deep

Sharks, rays, and chimaeras are predators that skillfully hunt, attack, and eat their prey. One of the reasons they are such successful hunters is that they have super senses. In addition to having great eyesight, their sense of smell is very impressive. Many sharks can smell just one drop of blood out of a billion drops of water. Now there's a good reason never to go swimming with a cut finger! Recent research by Dr. John Maisey at the American Museum of Natural History in New York City has shown that both living and extinct sharks have a heightened sense of hearing. They can hear ultralow frequencies of sound and can tell what direction it is coming from.

Extra Senses

Sharks have the same five senses as humans: taste, touch, sight, hearing, and smell. The extraordinary thing is that they have two extra senses beyond that. Fish can feel small vibrations in the water. They have two sensitive lines that run down the sides of their bodies, called lateral lines. These sensory lines help them feel pressure changes in the water caused by other fishes swimming nearby.

Sharks, rays, and chimaeras have another sense that's even more astounding—electroreception. They can sense their prey through electricity. Even if a shark can't see or smell its prey, it can sense the subtle electrical charge all animals make.

It's as if sharks have a built-in radar detector.

If you look closely at the nose of a shark you'll see it's covered with black holes. These are called ampullae (am-POO-lay) of Lorenzini (named after the guy who discovered them in the 1600s); they are the shark's electrical receptors, helping it to feel the "buzz" of any living thing near it. Some scientists think this is why the kidney-headed (or hammerhead) shark has such a broad head: because it's helpful to have electrical receptors spread across a wide area. When you think about it, kidney-headed sharks *do* look a lot like those metal detectors you see folks using at the beach.

There is one more thing that makes sharks such successful hunters. Teeth. And lots of them.

Tooth-making Machines

For every kind of shark there is a different kind of tooth. Open-ocean hunters have razor-sharp teeth with serrated edges that can cut through flesh like a steak knife. Bottom-dwelling, ambush predators like the goblin shark have long narrow teeth for snagging prey that swim near them. Guitarfish have rounded, flat teeth for cracking open clam shells.

And when old teeth wear out, new ones move in to replace them. Sharks have row upon row of teeth, and new ones are constantly forming at the back of the mouth. The back teeth move forward into position as the front teeth fall out. Some shark species produce as many as 20,000 teeth in their lifetime! That's why shark teeth are the most commonly found vertebrate fossil. Sharks must really keep the tooth fairy busy. And just think: sharks never need false teeth.

Prickly Personalities

Believe it or not, a shark's skin is made from thousands of little teeth! Well, almost. The shark's skin scales (called denticles) are nearly identical to the teeth found in their mouths. That's why shark skin is so rough it can even be used as sandpaper. Just rubbing the skin of some sharks can actually cut you!

Sharks vs. Humans

Sharks have been swimming in the oceans for a long, long time. They have survived many global extinctions that have killed off entire groups of animals from the Earth. They've outlived the ancient trilobites, ammonites, and even the giant dinosaurs. Yet today many of these magnificent predators face the greatest enemy in their history—humans.

Each year about 100 people are attacked by sharks around the world. Only around 10 of those people die. That's a very small number when you realize that every year, lightning, bees, pigs, and even Christmas tree lights kill more humans than sharks do.

But look at it from the shark's point of view. Humans kill millions of sharks every year. Large fleets of industrial fishing boats catch sharks for food or accidentally kill them while fishing for other species. Often, sharks are killed just for their fins to make shark-fin soup. Sometimes the fins are removed while the shark is still alive and then it's tossed overboard to die a slow death.

Sharks reproduce slowly. Many species are on the brink of extinction. Since most sharks live in the open ocean, laws protecting them are hard to enforce. If we want future generations to appreciate the astounding variety of sharks living today, we must all work together to save them.

Of the 18 living sharks in this book, only 1 can be considered dangerous to humans: the bull shark. Great white sharks, tiger sharks, mako sharks, sand tiger sharks, requiem sharks, and blacktip sharks are also high on the list for recorded shark attacks. River rays and stingarees can inflict painful wounds if accidentally stepped on. We can only speculate about the danger level of extinct sharks. This much is certain though: I would never have wanted to be in the water when megalodon was around!

Depending on a shark's size and other factors, prey includes sea mammals such as whales, sea turtles, other sharks, fish, crustaceans, mollusks, worms and other invertebrates, and plankton. Larger sharks are preyed on by other sharks, killer whales, and humans. Smaller sharks are eaten by bigger fish, marine mammals, squid, and humans.

Sharks have 3 different kinds of reproductive systems: oviparous (oh-vee-VIP-air-us)—producing eggs that hatch within the body of the parent female, where there is no placental connection; oviparous (oh-VIP-air-us)—producing eggs that hatch after being ejected by the female; and viviparous (vy-VIP-air-us)— producing live young within the body of the parent female. To simplify, you could say that sharks either give birth to live babies or produce eggs. Overall facts on frequency of birth are not readily available: most sharks have young about every 2 years, and some sharks, like kidney-headed sharks, have young yearly. Sharks have from 1 to 28 pups in a litter.

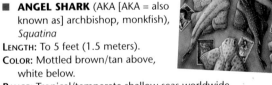

- **ANGEL SHARK** (AKA [AKA = also known as] archbishop, monkfish), *Squatina*
  LENGTH: To 5 feet (1.5 meters).
  COLOR: Mottled brown/tan above, white below.
  RANGE: Tropical/temperate shallow seas worldwide.
  REMARKS: There are about 14 different species of angel shark. This flat shark buries itself in sand with only its eyes poking out and waits for fish to pass over. It then bursts out at lightning speed and inhales its prey.
  STATUS: Abundant on the North Pacific Coast, but some populations are under stress from overfishing.

- **BULL SHARK** (AKA cub shark, Ganges shark, river whaler, Lake Nicaragua shark, Zambezi shark), *Carcharhinus leucas*
  LENGTH: To 11.5 feet (3.5 meters).
  COLOR: Brownish gray above, white below.
  RANGE: Tropical/subtropical seas; ventures into freshwater rivers and lakes.
  REMARKS: Unlike other sharks, the bull shark can live in both saltwater and freshwater. It has been found 1,800 miles up the Mississippi River and 3,000 miles up the Amazon. In Costa Rica it breeds in Lake Nicaragua, regularly migrating 100 miles up the San Juan River. It is aggressive and is one of the most dangerous sharks of all. It was a bull shark that attacked 8-year-old Jessie Arbogast in the summer of 2001, severing his arm and setting off a nationwide wave of elasmophobia (an unusual fear of sharks).
  STATUS: Some populations are nearly extinct due to fishing. The Lake Nicaragua bull shark has been virtually eliminated.

- **COOKIE-CUTTER SHARK** (AKA luminous shark, cigar shark), *Isistius brasiliensis*
  LENGTH: 1.5 feet (45.7 centimeters).
  COLOR: Dark brown above, tan below, a dark band around the gill slits, and fins have a whitish transparent edge.
  RANGE: Global in temperate/tropical seas.
  REMARKS: This diabolical little shark belongs to the dogfish family. For years, fishermen were puzzled by the round cookie-size bite marks on the tuna and marlin they caught, and scientists also saw the same mysterious holes on the sides of dolphins and whales. The most perplexing cases were when submarines returned to their bases with perfectly round holes all over their rubberized hulls. Finally, scientists figured out that this shark uses its large lips and sharp triangular teeth like a toothy suction cup to pull circular cookie-size chunks of flesh out of its prey. Once attached to its victim, it sucks tightly and swivels in a quick circular movement to remove its meal. Its eyes and belly glow an eerie green color, which lures big predatory fish and sea mammals in. Once they're close enough, this sneaky little shark turns the table and attacks the attacker.
  STATUS: Unknown.

- **DOGFISH** (AKA spiny dogfish, spurdogs, piked dogfish), *Squalus acanthias* and *Somniosus pacificus*
  LENGTH: Members of the dogfish family range from the tiny 7-inch-long dwarf dogshark to the colossal 25-foot-long Pacific sleeper shark. Spiny dogfish reach 5.5 feet in length (1.6 meters).
  COLOR: Usually grayish brown above, lighter below.
  RANGE: Global; spiny dogfish and sleeper sharks are found in colder seas.
  REMARKS: The common name "dogfish" refers to an entire order of sharks (Squaliformes) with 3 families and about 84 species. There are 2 species shown on pages 8–9: *Squalus acanthias* is shown in the foreground. Lurking in the distance is the gigantic Pacific sleeper shark (*Somniosus pacificus*). The spiny dogfish shown in the illustration is an important food source in many countries; the English prize them for fish and chips. It may be the most numerous shark in the seas. Traditionally the dogfish is an important clan symbol for many Native American groups on the Pacific Northwest Coast, and appears on carved totems and masks. It may also be one of the most long-lived of shark species, some reaching a ripe old age of 70 years. The Pacific sleeper shark is arguably the largest living predatory shark.
  STATUS: Common in many areas, but overharvesting has taken a severe toll on some populations due to their slow reproduction rate.

- **ELEPHANTFISH** (AKA ghost shark, plownose chimaera, whitefish), *Callorhinchus*
  LENGTH: To 3.6 feet (1.09 meters).
  COLOR: Silvery above with dark brown blotches on sides, white below.
  RANGE: 3 species are found in temperate seas off Australia, South America, and Africa.
  REMARKS: One of the most primitive of chondrichthyans. This chimaera is found in the southern oceans. Fossils of similar forms date back 325 million years. It is fished commercially in New Zealand and Australia. Chimaeras

are named after an infamous fire-breathing monster from Greek mythology that had the head of a lion, the body of a goat, and a snake for a tail. They are also commonly called ratfish because of their long rat-like tail. I am especially fond of these bizarre fish that look like a science experiment gone wrong.

STATUS: Common within the range, but commercial fishing's effect should be closely monitored.

■ FRILLED SHARK (AKA frill shark, frill-gilled shark), *Chlamydoselachus anguineus*

LENGTH: 6.6 feet (2 meters).
COLOR: Dark brown all over.
RANGE: Deep water worldwide, but patchy distribution.

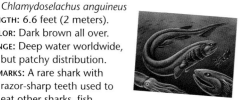

REMARKS: A rare shark with razor-sharp teeth used to eat other sharks, fish, octopus, and squid. It has 6 gill slits (most sharks have only 5) that are large and extend nearly around its snake-like head. The gill slits have ridges that look like frills, which give them their name.
STATUS: Unknown.

■ GOBLIN SHARK (AKA elfin shark, hobgoblin shark, imp shark), *Mitsukurina owstoni*

LENGTH: 12.8 feet (3.9 meters).
COLOR: Pinkish gray.
RANGE: Deep water worldwide.
REMARKS: First discovered off the coast of Japan in 1898, and only 45 have been caught since! Little is known about this extremely rare, strange-looking shark. Its large nose is covered with ampullae of Lorenzini, so it most likely hunts its prey by detecting their electrical fields. Its jaws can protrude quickly to make a fast kill.
STATUS: Unknown.

■ HELICOPRION (AKA whorl-toothed shark, buzz-saw shark), *Helicoprion*

LENGTH: Estimated to about 20 feet (6 meters).
COLOR: Unknown.
RANGE: Global—fossils have been found in the United States (Idaho, Wyoming, and Nevada), Japan, Australia, and Iran.
REMARKS: There are about 6 described species. Known from a bizarre whorl of teeth first described by Russian paleontologist A. P. Karpinsky in 1899, who spent the

better part of his life trying to understand exactly how this whorl was used. In many amusing reconstructions he placed the whorl on the upper jaw, protruding from the back, and even dangling from the tail. The mystery was not solved until 1966, when Dr. Svend Erik Bendix-Almgreen from Denmark studied well-preserved specimens from Idaho that had traces of the skull structure and jaws. He figured out that the whorl was positioned in the lower jaw and was used for attacking prey. There are only tiny crushing teeth on the upper jaws. The makeup of the rear half of the body is not known.
STATUS: Extinct. Lived during the Permian period 225 to 280 million years ago.

■ INIOPTERYGIAN (AKA iniops, flying shark), *Iniopterygian*

LENGTH: To about 1.5 feet (45 centimeters).
COLOR: Unknown.
RANGE: Fossils found in Indiana, Illinois, Nebraska, and Montana.
REMARKS: These small, big-eyed chondrichthyans were very unusual in that they had their large pectoral fins positioned on the upper part of their body attached to their neck. The name "Iniopterygian" means "neck fin." There is an undetermined number of families in this order. The illustration for letter "I" shows 10 species. They have a basic similarity to modern-day flying fishes.
STATUS: Extinct. Lived during the Mississippian and Pennsylvanian periods from 345 to 280 million years ago.

■ JAPANESE DEVILRAY (AKA devilfish), *Mobula japonica*

LENGTH: 10.2 feet across (3.1 meters).
COLOR: Dark bluish above, silver gray around the eyes, white below.
RANGE: Tropical seas worldwide.
REMARKS: This gigantic ray is a filter feeder that performs graceful maneuvers as it feeds on plankton, looping in circles through the seas. It also performs spectacular leaps, rocketing up out of the water and landing with a loud smack on its belly. Its larger cousin, the manta ray, is 22 feet (6.7 meters) across and performs the same maneuvers. It even does somersaults. They may do these tricks to dislodge parasites or as a signal to

other devilrays. Perhaps they do it because it just looks cool.
STATUS: Common in open tropical oceans.

■ KIDNEY-HEADED SHARK (AKA scalloped hammerhead), *Sphryna lewini*

LENGTH: 13 feet (4 meters).
COLOR: Brownish gray above, paler below.
RANGE: Tropical seas worldwide.
REMARKS: This shark is the most common and widely distributed of the 9 species of hammerhead sharks. Known in the U.S. as the scalloped hammerhead, this species has indentations on its wide head that look a little like the edge of a scallop shell. Elsewhere the head reminds people of a kidney shape. Different theories have been put forth about why its head is shaped like a wedge: it helps with vision, adds lift for swimming, increases the sense of smell, and gives a wider area for electro-sensing, and all may be true. Kidney-headed sharks sometimes gather by the hundreds in large migratory schools.
STATUS: Fairly common, but its numbers are declining.

■ LISTRACANTHUS (AKA porcupine eel shark), *Listracanthus histrix*

LENGTH: Unknown but probably quite large.
COLOR: Unknown.
RANGE: Fossils found in Indiana, Illinois, Iowa, and Montana.
REMARKS: For decades fossil hunters have found thousands upon thousands of long, feathery denticles (teeth-like formations) of *Listracanthus* in the black shale deposits of the Midwest. Some are more than 4 inches long. Occasionally large clumps are found, indicating the shark was covered with these things. Dr. Rainer Zangerl once found a large slab that revealed a long shark body covered with thousands of spiky denticles, but as luck would have it the rock literally crumbled to dust when it dried out, so all we have is a great "fish story" about the big one that got away. Scientists now think that another species called *Petrodus* (known only from round denticles) may actually be the belly skin of this elusive beast.
STATUS: Extinct. Lived during the Mississippian and Pennsylvanian periods from 345 to 280 million years ago.

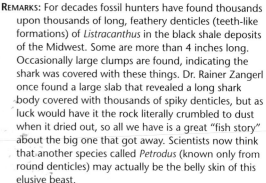

- **MEGALODON** (AKA megatooth shark), *Carcharodon megalodon* or *Carcharocles megalodon*

LENGTH:
Approximately
60 feet
(18.75 meters).
COLOR: Unknown.
RANGE: Fossils found
worldwide.

REMARKS: This enormous shark was perhaps the largest predator that ever lived on this planet, outweighing even the mighty *T-rex* by several tons. Scientists still debate whether it was a direct ancestor of today's great white shark or if it was more closely related to mako sharks. Either way it was one fearsome shark that could easily have swallowed a Volkswagen Beetle for lunch. The teeth of megalodon alone are up to 7 inches long and are found around the world. For comparison, the long-nosed dolphins on the right in the illustration on pages 20–21 are about 6 feet long, or about the height of your dad.

STATUS: Extinct. Lived from the Miocene to the Pliocene epoch, 3 to 25 million years ago.

- **NURSE SHARK,** *Ginglymostoma cirratum*

LENGTH: To 13.1 feet (4 meters).
COLOR: Yellowish brown above, paler below.
RANGE: In the Atlantic Ocean from Rhode Island to Brazil, in the Pacific Ocean from Baja to Peru.
REMARKS: There are different stories about how this shark's common name came to be. One version says that the name comes from the loud sucking sound the shark makes when it's brought onboard a boat, much like a nursing baby. Another story says it's derived from this shark's habit of lying around in heaps on the ocean floor looking like a bunch of nursing puppies or kittens. The nurse shark has whiskers that help it find prey hiding between rocks or in the sand. When it does find a tasty morsel it uses that sucking ability to inhale its meal. Unlike most other sharks it can remain motionless on the bottom and can pump water over its gills.

STATUS: Common, routinely encountered by divers.

- **ORNITHOPRION** (AKA bony-probe shark), *Ornithoprion*

LENGTH: Estimated to 2 feet (60 centimeters).
COLOR: Unknown.

RANGE: Fossils found in Illinois and Indiana.
REMARKS: This small, big-eyed shark had an unusually long skull and a long probe on its lower jaw. The probe was composed of hard bone-like material, which is unusual for a cartilaginous fish. Ornithoprion also had a half-whorl of flat, crushing teeth, indicating that it was related to Helicoprion. Only the head and shoulder parts have ever been found.

STATUS: Extinct. Lived during the Pennsylvanian period 325 to 280 million years ago.

- **PETALODONT** (AKA petal-toothed shark, artichoke-toothed shark), *Petalodont*

LENGTH: Petalodonts vary greatly in size. The species portrayed on page 22 is up to 15 inches (38 centimeters).
COLOR: Unknown.
RANGE: Ancient Montana and Indiana (other Petalodonts are found around the world).
REMARKS: This ancient order of sharks had many species. The shark illustrated on page 22 is *Belantsea montana.* It was found by Dr. Richard Lund at the world-famous fossil site of Bear Gulch in Montana in the mid-1980s. This strange shark must have been a slow-moving reef dweller. It may have used its big teeth to gnaw on coral or sponge colonies.

STATUS: Extinct; *Belantsea montana* lived during Mississippian times 345 to 325 million years ago. Other Petalodonts flourished during the Mississippian and Pennsylvanian periods and vanished by the end of the Permian period 225 million years ago.

- **QUEENSLAND SAWFISH** (AKA dwarf sawfish), *Pristis clavata*

LENGTH: To 5 feet (1.5 meters).
COLOR: Greenish brown above, white below.
RANGE: Known from Australian waters.
REMARKS: There are about 7 species of sawfish in the world, some of which grow to the incredible length of 23 feet. The species on page 23 grows to at least 5 feet. Sawfish are a highly modified kind of ray with long, spiked snouts. They thrash their formidable saw-shaped schnozzes back and forth rapidly to stun and maim their prey. Sawfish can enter freshwater river systems just like bull sharks do, and are often found hundreds of miles from the ocean. Many breed in freshwater.

STATUS: Many sawfish populations are in steep decline due to overfishing and habitat loss.

- **RIVER RAY** (AKA freshwater stingray), *Paratrygon, Plesiotrygon, Potamotrygon*

LENGTH: Most river rays are about 12 to 18 inches across (30 to 45 centimeters), but Paratrygon can be up to 60 inches across (152 centimeters).
COLOR: Wide variety of camouflage patterns.
RANGE: Freshwater river systems of northern South America.
REMARKS: There are about 20 species of South American freshwater river rays, or stingrays, with more than 50 varieties of color patterns. Most are found in the Amazon River basin and belong to the 3 genera. Feared more by locals than piranha, people can become sick for days from the river ray's sting. The enzyme on the poisonous barb can cause muscle tissue to dissolve, which is very painful. If the wound is not treated properly, death is a possibility. River rays are the only chondrichthyans to live their entire lives in freshwater. They have evolved from stingrays that once inhabited the oceans but were eventually cut off from saltwater a long time ago.

STATUS: Common throughout northern South America, some of the more exotically colored species are popular in the aquarium trade and wild populations should be monitored.

- **SCISSOR-TOOTHED SHARK,** *Edestus*

LENGTH: This species to about 12 feet (3.75 meters).
COLOR: Unknown.
RANGE: Probably global.
REMARKS: There are a number of species in the genus

Edestus, some ranging to huge proportions. The species shown on page 26 is *Edestus heinrichi*. Scissor-toothed sharks flourished in the great age of sharks during the Paleozoic era. These sharks were probably fast open-ocean predators. First discovered in 1855, scientists are only now coming to understand how their jaws worked. Recent discoveries have revealed upper and lower teeth fossilized in place along with some skull material, giving a better indication of their appearance in life. One specimen, *Edestus giganteus,* at the American Museum of Natural History in New York, is huge: it sports 3-inch-long teeth. Amazingly it's the only fossil of this monster ever found.

STATUS: Extinct. Lived during the Pennsylvanian period 325 to 280 million years ago.

■ **THRESHER SHARK**
(AKA bigeye thresher), *Alopias superciliosus*
LENGTH: 15 feet (4.5 meters).
COLOR: Purplish gray above, white below.
RANGE: Global in warm seas.
REMARKS: The 3 species of thresher sharks all have enormously long tails that make up half their body length. The thresher shark uses its tail like a giant baseball bat, swinging it wildly through schools of fish. The victims are stunned senseless, and the hungry shark quickly gobbles them up. Some thresher sharks also use their big tails to launch themselves out of the water in spectacular leaps.
STATUS: Populations are under severe stress from overfishing.

■ **UROLOPHUS STINGAREE** (AKA stingaree, round stingray), *Urolophus*
LENGTH: Ranges from 10 to 30 inches (25 to 76 centimeters), depending on the species.
COLOR: Highly variable, usually mottled above, white below.

RANGE: Most species are found in Australian waters, with another found from Panama to northern California.
REMARKS: The stingaree resembles a stingray but has a shorter tail with a bigger tail fin. *Urolophus* is the genus name for this group, which has about 15 species in it. This ray is relatively small but can pack a powerful wallop with its barbed stingers. Since it is small, it's unlikely that it has caused death. Although it uses its tail stingers purely as a defensive weapon, it has sometimes been observed swimming backward toward a possible threat.
STATUS: Fairly common in near-shore areas within their range.

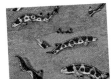

■ **VARIED CARPET SHARK**
(AKA necklace carpet shark, varied cat shark), *Parascyllium variolatum*
LENGTH: To 3 feet (91 centimeters).
COLOR: White spots against brown background, with dark band around neck region.
RANGE: South coast of Australia.
REMARKS: There are 7 species of carpet sharks. They are shy reef dwellers rarely seen in daylight, coming out at night to forage for food in rocky crevices.
STATUS: Unknown.

■ **WHALE SHARK** (AKA tofu shark), *Rhincodon typus*
LENGTH: To 46 feet (14 meters).
COLOR: Bluish gray/brown above, with rows of creamy white spots, white below.
RANGE: Global in tropical seas.

REMARKS: The whale shark is the world's largest living fish. It glides gracefully through the ocean depths with its huge mouth agape, inhaling clouds of tiny creatures for food. Whale sharks have 300 rows of tiny teeth lining their jaws. Scuba divers once hitched rides on these gentle giants by grabbing onto a fin, but now this practice is frowned on as it may upset or even harm the shark. Despite their great size, whale sharks have been kept successfully in public aquariums. They may live to be more than 100 years old.
STATUS: Unknown. Researchers fear their numbers are diminishing rapidly. Because of their large size, whale sharks are vulnerable to any changes in the ocean food chain. They have been heavily hunted for their mild flesh similar to tofu.

■ **XENACANTH SHARK** (AKA Texas swamp shark), *Xenacanth*
LENGTH: To 10 feet (3 meters).
COLOR: Unknown.
RANGE: Worldwide; the most complete fossils come from Germany and Texas.
REMARKS: Xenacanth sharks were an order of freshwater sharks. The species shown on page 31 is called *Orthacanthus*. It evolved a

form that would allow great maneuverability in narrow wood-clogged streams and lakes. Most likely it was an ambush predator that waited for an unlucky victim to venture near.

Its wide, snake-like mouth full of double-pronged teeth was ideal for snagging and holding prey tight. The *Xenacanth* shark sported wicked-looking head spines used as protection from other predators.
STATUS: Extinct. *Orthacanthus* lived during the Permian period from 325 to 280 million years ago. The *Xenacanth* shark order disappeared during the Triassic period about 200 million years ago. *Xenacanth* sharks were one of the longest-lived groups of chondrichthyans on Earth, having evolved beginning in the Devonian period and surviving until they disappeared in the Triassic period, roughly 150 million years ago.

■ **YELLOW SHOVELNOSE GUITARFISH** (AKA southern shovelnose ray, western shovelnose ray), *Aptychotrema vincentiana*
LENGTH: To 32 inches (80 centimeters).

COLOR: Yellowish brown above with dark brown blotches, white below.
RANGE: Coastal waters of Australia.
REMARKS: Guitarfish are actually a kind of modified ray. There are approximately 43 species of shovelnose guitarfish in the world, with most of them occurring in the Western Pacific. The largest guitarfish reach a length of 6 feet. They are bottom-dwelling shallow-water denizens and prefer sandy sea bottoms where they can use their shovel-like snouts to dig up clams and crustaceans and crack them open with their flattened grinding teeth.
STATUS: Common within their range.

■ **ZEBRA SHARK** (AKA leopard shark), *Stegastoma fasciatum*
LENGTH: To 11.5 feet (3.5 meters).
COLOR: Brownish yellow above with numerous dark brown spots, whitish below. Juveniles have dark vertical bars against a yellowish background.
RANGE: Tropical waters of the Indian and Western Pacific Oceans.
REMARKS: The adult zebra shark is regal looking, with elegant jaguar spots and a long flowing tail. It is a somewhat sluggish creature that becomes more active at night. It is seen perched on rocky lookouts below the waves, quietly pumping water over its gills, checking out the scene around it.
STATUS: Common within its range.

FOR MORE ON SHARKS, LOOK FOR THESE GREAT BOOKS:

The Book of Sharks, by Richard Ellis, Harcourt Brace Jovanovich, 1983.

Reef Sharks & Rays of the World, by Scott W. Michael, Sea Challengers Press, 1993.

Shark!, by Jeffrey L. Rottman, Ipso Facto Press, 1999.

The Shark Almanac, by Thomas B. Allen, Lyons Press, 1999.

Sharks and Rays, Nature Company Guides, edited by Leighton Taylor, The Nature Company & Time-Life Books, 1997.

Sharks and Rays of Australia, by P. R. Last & J. D. Stevens, CSIRO, Australia, 1994.

Sharks and Rays of the World, by Doug Perrine, Voyageur Press, 1999.

Sharks in Question, The Smithsonian Answer Book, by Victor G. Springer and Joy P. Gold, Smithsonian Institution Press, 1989.

Library of Congress Cataloging-in-Publication Data:
Troll, Ray, 1954–
     Sharkabet : a sea of sharks from A to Z.
        p.   cm.
     ISBN 1-55868-518-9 (hb)
     ISBN 1-55868-519-7 (sb)
     1. Sharks—Miscellanea. 2. Sharks—Pictorial works. 3. Chondrichthyes—Miscellanea.
     4. English language—Alphabet. I. Title.
QL638.9 .T76 2001
597.3—dc21

                                              2001046528

Printed in Singapore

WestWinds Press®
An imprint of Graphic Arts Center Publishing Company
P.O. Box 10306, Portland, Oregon 97296-0306
503-226-2402
www.gacpc.com
President: Charles M. Hopkins
Associate Publisher: Douglas A. Pfeiffer
Editorial Staff: Timothy W. Frew, Tricia Brown, Kathy Matthews, Jean Andrews, Jean Bond-Slaughter
Production Staff: Richard L. Owsiany, Susan Dupere
Editor: Ellen Wheat
Photographer: John Wolon
Designer: Elizabeth Watson

The original full-color art for the book was created using a variety of media on black Somerset paper, 22 x 27 inches. Media included colored pencils, oil crayons, oil pastels, and occasionally air-brushed acrylic paints. For more information on Ray Troll and his phenomenally fishy art, go to the Internet, www.trollart.com

I'm very grateful to all of the experts who gave me advice on this book. Any mistakes are purely my own. The occasional lapses in the laws of gravity and the odd combination of sharks with things like school buses and kidney bean cans can be blamed on my overactive imagination. May the reality police forgive me. And kids, please remember that while it may look like tons of fun to go swimming with the sharks, they can be very, very dangerous.
                                              —R. T.

ON THE COVER: The ferocious-looking shark devouring the letters on the cover of the book (also seen on pages 1 and 4) is the notorious great white shark, *Carcharodon carcharias*. Immortalized in the *Jaws* movies, the great white shark prefers a diet of seals, sea lions, and dead whales. It can reach 21 feet in length and can weigh more than 3 tons. Like several other sharks, it can protrude its upper jaws in a nasty-looking grimace when delivering a fatal bite. Researchers fear that the great white shark is in real danger of extinction.

SHARKABET

FOR RAINER AND DICK, TWO PALEO-SHARK HUNTERS WHO CHANGED MY LIFE

Thanks to: My family (Michelle, Patrick, and Corinna) for encouraging and tolerating my love of sharks, Patrick for the idea, Dr. Rainer Zangerl, Dr. Dick Lund, Dr. Eileen Grogan, Dr. John Maisey, "Stingray" Andrew Camoens, Dr. Dominique Didier Dagit, the ratfish queen, Dr. Carl "Catfish" Ferraris, Dr. Gordon Hubbell, Dr. Mike Gottfried, Dr. Philippe Janvier, Dr. Svend Erik Bendix-Almgreen, Dr. J. D. Stewart, Dr. John McCosker, Richard Ellis, Dave Ebert, Elda Brizuela, Cliff Jeremiah, Adrienne Cuiffo, Terry Ketler, Stephen Peters, Brad Matsen, Ratfish Russ Wodehouse, Marlene Blessing, Deborah Loop, and ALL the highly evolved bony fish at Graphic Arts Center Publishing Co., especially Ellen and Betty.
                                              —R. T.